# dawning of the new beard

ISBN 978-0-8341-2511-7

themosaicexperiment.com

Printed in the United States of America

Cover and Interior Design by Arthur Cherry
Cover Illustration by Keith Alexander

10 9 8 7 6 5 4 3 2 1

# the mosaic experiment
Bringing Old Testament Practices Out of Retirement
Wendie Brockhaus / Lucas Cole / Padraic Ingle / Brian Schafer

**The House Studio**, Kansas City, Missouri

# Contents

**We would *never***
put an introduction in a book

**Mo·sa·ic** / mō—ʻzā—ik

**1.** of or relating to Moses; writings attributed to him **2.** a surface decoration made by inlaying small pieces of variously colored material to form pictures **3.** awesomeness in a book

One day during a House Studio coffee break, we were talking about the sudden overgrowth of hipsters . . .

Which led us to talking about a web site called Whiskerino (whiskerino.org), consisting of a bunch of guys who document their unruly beard growth . . .

Which led to us talking about how Moses would have been an epic candidate for Whiskerino . . .

Which led us to talking about how weird it is that Christians often pretend like the Old Testament doesn't exist . . .

Which led to this book.

We're sure you see how it all correlates.

Facial hair, compelling as it may be, isn't the only reason we started this project.

See, we're slightly over (bored to tears with) small group curriculum that tells us all the "right" answers and sums up our faith in five bullet.points. We don't think following Christ is clean or cute. We refuse to fill in any more blanks. And it feels a little redundant to meet once a week just to sit, talk, and eat fruit pizza . . . until next week when we will inevitably do it all over again, give or take the dessert. (But preferably *give*, right?)

Even so, the snarky deconstruction thing is way overdone—criticism doesn't accomplish much by itself. Instead, we wanted to spend our energy on creating a different way for faith communities to engage the Good Text and one another.

We call it uncurriculum, but you can call it whatever you want. (See definition 3 at the beginning for suggestions.)

*The Mosaic Experiment* is a book that revisits some of those ancient, Old Testament practices that are still relevant to kingdom living in the twenty-first century.

Truth is, there's a lot we don't get about the first half of the Bible

(Granted, we haven't exactly aced the second half.) But it all matters for some reason. I mean, who picks up a book and starts reading from the middle? There's something important about those first few chapters—character development, for instance. Like, who is this God who is fine to go by "I Am"? And what is he up to in the world?

This book is called *The Mosaic Experiment* because all of its themes are found in the first five books of the Bible—the Pentateuch.

Some smart people say that Moses wrote the Pentateuch. Other smart people say he didn't write the whole thing. We don't know because Moses didn't come to us for his publishing. (Probably went with Zondervan, and we're only slightly bitter.)

"Mosaic" also seems to fit in an artistic sense. (See definition 2 at the beginning.) The themes you'll find in the next few chapters are meaningful, yet eclectic—just small pieces of a much larger picture: pilgrimage, altar building, scapegoats, cities of refuge. They aren't the only themes in the Pentateuch, maybe not even the most important. And we know we don't own the market on which OT rituals stay or go, but these are just a few that grabbed our attention. You know, turned on the lights for us.

Something to be aware of—the Pentateuch was written in the pre-modern era during a time when people used narrative not only to remember and pass on important truth but to engage imagination. It's a collection of writing genres that include mythopoetic (Genesis 1-11), folk narrative, law, poetry, etc. So to approach these writings with a scientific, modern mindset may work against you. Moses wasn't trying to establish a religion or leave behind secret formulas for righteousness that we would later have to decode.

A lot happened in the first five books of the Bible. Beginning with Adam and Eve in a garden and ending four books later when the tired Israelite nation is finally ready to cross into their promised land after a small 40-year detour. Everything in between is a matter of us getting to know a holy and untamed God who proves he will stop at nothing to be in covenant relationship with humanity.

From a cosmic and local creation account to a cosmic and local redemption account, we imagine hearing it all straight from the mouth of Moses—our musky, old grandpa who seems to know a good sweater vest when he sees one and can tell a story like no one else.

Maybe it goes without saying, but we think vintage is making a comeback.

let's
begin
here

We know you hate directions. But you can always tear this page out and find your own way through the book.

# it's plain and simple.

**1 Read and discuss a chapter.**

2  Each person choose one of
seven experiments to carry out . . .
or make up some of your own.

**3 Journal your thoughts on our
pages. (Why else would we give
you so much white space?)**

4  Share your stories with the
group next week.

the
garden

Genesis 2:15

Adam was the first farmer. Before any improper fruit eating or fig leaf clothing, the first human was commissioned to look after his very own backyard. And yet it's a lot easier to think of something like working the earth and tilling soil as punishment (a prehistoric sitting in the corner) for Adam and Eve's huge disobedience. God did say, "Cursed is the ground because of you; through painful toil you will eat of it all the days of your life" (Genesis 3:17b).

But let's rewind.

God wasn't trying to correct anything when he told Adam to work and care for the earth. It was his original intention for the first human to "go green" before there was any such thing as sin or disobedience in the Garden. **"The LORD God took the man and put him in the Garden of Eden to work it and take care of it" (Genesis 2:15).** For God, humans looking after the environment was one part of picture-perfect creation.

*This* is how it was supposed to be.

Since the very beginning of the story humans were set apart from other animals or plants. God made us to reflect his creative image so we might fill the earth, be responsible for it, reproduce, and subdue it. The whole idea of being intricately and actively involved in the creating process—it's central to our humanity.

But there's one big problem at this point. Since the beginning we've chosen our own way, which makes it impossible for us to get in on God's vision—even on matters of good ecology. Our sin has resulted in a very different garden than the one God had imagined.

Now we find ourselves in a world of factories and fast-food, and very few of us actually work or care for the earth in any capacity. Where once people lived by the rhythms of the natural world (for example rising and retiring with the sun), we can now go weeks without venturing outside of our artificial environments.

Urbanization and technology have given us more efficient ways of unplugging from creation and our original source, the Creator. We're disconnected.

The implications are huge. Not only does the earth suffer under our neglect; we do too. Our struggle to connect with the very thing God gave us to sustain our lives—the earth—inevitably disconnects us from him even further . . .

And there's more to the story. We see throughout the Old Testament that the Hebrew word for work or serve (*avad*) is from the same root as the Hebrew word for worship (*avodah*). God's desire for humans to care for creation isn't just about saving us from pollution and processed foods; it's also rooted in his desire for us to be in a worshipful, reverent relationship with him. To serve God's creation is one way to worship him and see him revealed.

When God told the first humans to work and care for the earth, he had a huge, beautiful picture in mind—not to act unilaterally but as a partnering God—so that humanity could join in on the creative work. Maybe you don't have a farm, or even a backyard for that matter. You're not exempt from the call to be a creative caretaker for this place. It's not like God is commanding you to go around hugging trees. Though let's be honest, there are a lot of worse things that could happen. God is asking that we use our creativity, energy, and time to look after the proverbial—or perhaps not so proverbial—Garden. It's right outside our door.

earth's
crammed with
heaven,
and every common
bush afire with
God; and only he
who sees takes off
his shoes,
the rest sit round
it and pluck
blackberries

**Elizabeth Barrett Browning**

Romans 8 talks about how the created world is waiting (groaning) in eager expectation for the sons of God to be revealed, in hopes that it will be liberated from decay. What does this mean for us? Does liberation (for both us and the earth) come during this life? Or only in the next?

**talk**

Maybe you live in an urban jungle, or don't have the option of working outside. Do you feel disconnected? Why or why not? How can you live in a way that doesn't leave you disconnected?

_____

# warning: your treadmill will talk smack.

Regular at a gym? Try an outdoor workout this week. Hike. Run. Walk someone's dog. Jump some rope. We don't care, just as long as you get some fresh air while you do your elevated heart rate thang.

**Pen, say hello to paper.**

# Where the Wild Things *Really* Are.

Many good things have come out of the ole' community camping trip. So many good things, in fact, it would be impossible for us to give you examples. But just trust us, it will be awesome.

**Drop a line.**

# Hold the double on the Whopper.

We enjoy a nice juicy burger ourselves, and yet consuming excessive amounts of meat is harmful to the environment and depletes the world food supply. So this week begin to cut back.

Consider this from the online magazine *GOOD*: "A study in *New Scientist* magazine reported that the production of one kilogram of beef produced as much greenhouse gasses as three hours of driving. The greenhouse gas emission of animals was calculated by considering the production and transportation of grain, as well as the methane emissions from animals.

If you're eating meat say four or five times a week, at 300 grams a go, there is 1.5 kilograms in a week. If you gave up that meat, you'd be decreasing your emissions by the same amount of 4.5 hours of driving."[1]

**Tell the page what you think.**

# word drop: eco-commons (people will think you're so smart.)

This experiment will require group collaboration. Get a master list going of original or recycled (pun definitely intended) ideas that can make you greener individuals and a greener faith community. Here are some thoughts to get you started: composting,,carpooling options, recycling programs at home and church, etc. We expect you'll be able to come up with some pretty cool ideas to share with us.

**White spaces are meant to be filled, says us.**

# Kind of like Super Wal-Mart, only the exact opposite.

Support your local farmer by making a trip to the farmer's market. As a way of planning ahead, ask questions about which produce you can expect throughout different seasons. By eating locally and seasonally, you cut back on the energy and emissions wasted in transport. Not to mention the fact that you'll be strengthening relationships with those in your community.

**Do tell.**

# No pressure. (Your shower is such a drain on the rest of us.)

Last year, UNICEF announced that humans need about five gallons of clean water a day to survive. The average per capita water use in the United States is 151 gallons per person per day—more than any other country in the world.[2]

A few good methods of reducing your water waste include: purchasing a low-pressure shower head, drinking from the tap rather than bottled waters, reducing coffee intake, lowering usage of lawn sprinkler systems, etc.

Watch this video for more ideas!
good.is/post/this-is-a-turn-off

**Save the ink industry. (Write things down.)**

# garden is the new grass. — says us the experts

We know your yard looks nice, but grass doesn't do much in the way of producing sustenance. Start a small community garden and plant a little extra so you can give it away to a local homeless shelter, rescue mission, or your hungry looking neighbor.

**Word. (that's right, we know slang)**

# Create your own experiment.

Push a pencil.

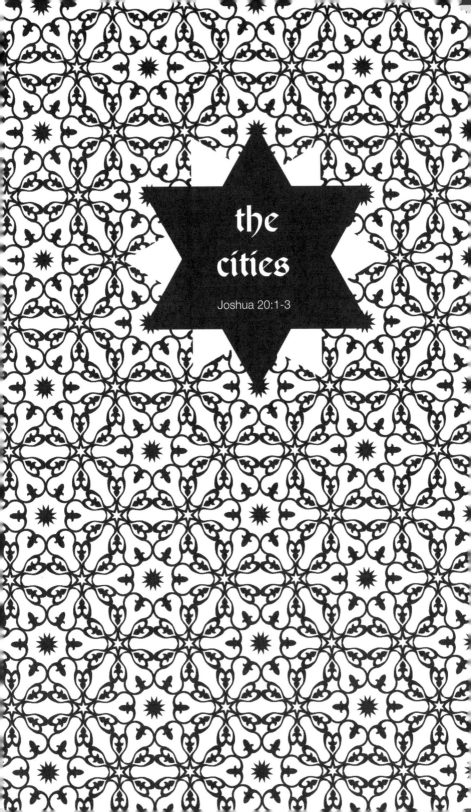

the

cities

Joshua 20:1-3

I have this tendency to personify the cities I visit. Each takes on a face of its own. Not to be stereotypical (but don't mind if I am), when I visit Chicago I expect deep-dish pizza, jazz clubs, and cab drivers who live for the Cubbies. Chicago is my black-wearing, culture-making, business friend. But upon entering Portland, give me bicycles instead of cabs and organic food stores instead of pizza joints. Portland is my green-living, coffee-drinking, hippie friend.

Landscapes aren't always the most distinguishable parts of a city, and often it's the people living in a city who give it strong and memorable features. The residents *are* the architecture.

That's why when God gave Israel the Promised Land, he had plans for the look and feel of the place. After all, his name was sort of attached to the real estate. And so he issued a set of rules, ways of living and being that would set his people apart. God had no desire for them to look like their neighbors or to keep up with the Joneses; instead, God's desire was for Israel to resemble himself, "a kingdom of priests and a holy nation" (Exodus 19:6). But what did it look like to be a nation in the image of God?

In Deuteronomy 19 (as well as Exodus 21:13, Numbers 35:9-15, and Deuteronomy 4:41-43), God issued a command for the Israelites to build cities (six cities, to be exact) where folks could escape if they had committed unintentional murder. These cities of refuge did not exempt a person from trial, but they clearly prohibited blood revenge prior to a trial. They functioned as asylums, safe places from possible retaliation by the offended.

And just in case Israel didn't hear him the first time, he reiterated his point to Joshua:

**"Then the LORD said to Joshua: Tell the Israelites to designate the**

**cities of refuge, as I instructed you through Moses, so that anyone who kills a person accidentally and unintentionally may flee there and find protection from the avenger of blood" (Joshua 20:1-3).**

A couple of things to note here.

We know Joshua isn't a part of the Pentateuch, but honestly we just like this translation better than the one in Deuteronomy.

Also, this kind of command would have been a big deal for people two thousand years ago. (Not that it's cake today.) But their systems of law looked a bit different. The due justice of that day was something like: You steal from me, I cut off your hands. You kill my brother, and I kill your whole family.

Yet we see in this Levitical law a call to perform justice in a way that looked alien to the world. To practice a redemption, reconciliation, and justice defined by God—not by the standard of the day. It is not too much of a leap to say that the people of God ultimately understood themselves as a whole to be a "city of refuge."

And what was true then is true now.

God still has a nation he expects to bear his image. In fact, he does some personifying himself, calling the Church his bride (John 3:29) and asking her to provide cities of refuge for those who are seeking redemption and reconciliation. Persons—even the guilty—do not have to live in fear of revenge taken against them (sounds a lot like 1 Cor. 13, don't you think?). To live among God's people is to live in a safe place, a city of refuge, where love trusts and believes to the very end.

we must learn to **regard people** less in the light of what they do or omit to do, and **more** in the light of what they suffer.

**Dietrich Bonhoeffer**

Imagine a modern city of refuge where everyone knows they've been given a second chance. How would that change the way people treat each other? Would it be better to live in a city of perfection? Why or why not?

talk

We no longer inhabit
land chosen by God for
his people. Therefore
our "cities" have to
take on a different look
than the ones in the Old
Testament. How has
the Church been (or not
been) a city of refuge
today? Who are the
people who need refuge
in our current context?

# We're kind of *Un*believable.

Cities of refuge for the offenders--and the offended.

In David Kinnaman and Gabe Lyon's book, *UnChristian*, a poll found that Christians are most commonly viewed as:

1 Hypocritical
2 Only focused on conversion
3 Anti-homosexual
4 Sheltered
5 Too political
6 Judgmental[3]

Pick one of these stereotypes to break this week, and tell us how you did it.

**Talk to me.**

# over you, spoon.

Cities of refuge for the doubting.

Host a doubt night in your small group or at your church. Give people a chance to air some of their doubts and concerns with faith in a safe place. Don't worry about spooning up all the answers; that's not what this is all about.

Consider making time at the end of the night to reflect on this statement: "Lord I believe, but help my unbelief" (Mark 9:24). Remind those who attend that God is not afraid of our hard questions or struggles with faith.

**Self-published = write in this book.**

# Justice looks so good on you, I think my glasses just broke.

Cities of refuge for the oppressed.

International Justice Mission (IJM) provides opportunities for you and your faith community to get involved with the hard issues of justice around the world. Go to their website (ijm.org) and look to see how you can get involved both individually and corporately.

**Drop a line.**

# Work gloves. Check. Trash bags. Check. Michael Jackson playlist on my iPod. Duh.

Cities of refuge for the graffiti'd.

This week spend time either in your church or in a neighborhood cleaning, removing graffiti, fixing up, or adding art. Beautify the place.

48

**Push a pencil.**

# How dr. phil of you.

Cities of refuge for the recovering.

Twelve-step programs have often been central places of transformation and relationship. In fact, the community and vulnerability within these groups are something the Church could really learn from.

Fill in the blank:
I am a recovering _____. (Shopaholic, legalist, liar, etc.)

Now, share with someone.

**Do tell.**

# Breaking news: God is not an American.

Cities of refuge for the foreigner.

Today, there are eighteen percent of people living in the United States for whom English is a second language. This week challenge yourself to engage in multi-cultural conversation. Or as a group, contact a non-English speaking church in your area and ask what kind of support they could most use.

**Send it.**

Toys (Good). Candy (Better). Toys made of candy (Awesome). Toys and candy that are capable of ruining furniture (The motherload).

Cities of refuge for the sick.

Many children suffering from chronic illness have to spend weeks or even months at a time in the hospital. Pediatric hospitals are great at providing care packages—toys, clothes, books, and goodies—for these kids. Contact your local hospital for care package guidelines.

**Pen, say hello to paper.**

# create your own experiment.

Tell the page what you think.

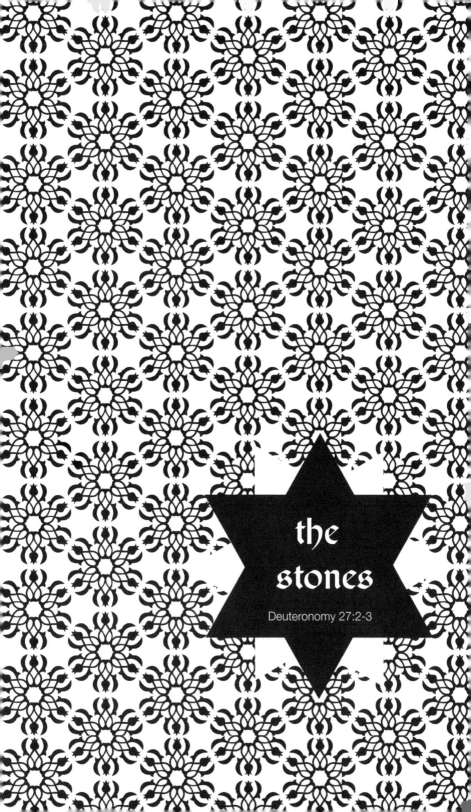

the
stones

Deuteronomy 27:2-3

**"When you have crossed the Jordan into the land the LORD your God is giving you, set up some large stones . . . Write on them all the words of this law when you have crossed over to enter the land the LORD your God is giving you, a land flowing with milk and honey, just as the LORD, the God of your fathers, promised you" (Deuteronomy 27:2-3).**

Have you ever forgotten something really important? The harder you tried to remember the more it seemed to elude you? And when you did manage to latch onto that lost memory rolling around in your skull, well, it was a bit dusty?

No, you say? Oh, me neither.

Remembering is a big part of our lives. We remember traditions, where we put our keys, and friends' birthdays. In fact, Post-it has built a corporate empire off miniature yellow notes designed to help us remember everything from our grocery list to little Johnny's soccer practice. Technology has only magnified the situation—phones and computers are constantly alerting us with due dates and appointment reminders. And while some individuals have the genius to memorize massive amounts of information like pi to six thousand decimal places (we don't know any of these people), everyone forgets things.

Which is okay. Except when forgetting means we begin to doubt God's faithfulness.

This was often the case for Israel, a nation who found itself on a long journey—wandering a desert wasteland for 40 years. Remembering was a critical part of their pilgrimage. Before they could answer, "Where are we going?" they first had to answer, "How did we get here?" Memory was vital to their movement. Their identity. Their future.

That's why in response to their spiritual amnesia, God's people made a practice of piling large rocks as monuments to the Lord's provision.

"In the future, when your children ask you, 'What do these stones mean?' tell them that the flow of the Jordan was cut off before the ark of the covenant of the LORD. When it crossed the Jordan, the waters of the Jordan were cut off. These stones are to be a memorial to the people of Israel forever" (Joshua 4:6b-7).

And here's the thing. God is still stopping rivers for us. Still acting miraculously on our behalf. Still taking us out of slavery and into something completely other.

He does phenomenal things every day and occasionally we even thank him, but as soon as trouble comes or a distraction arrives we lose sight of all the miracles and blessings, disciplines and progress that he brings.

Where are our rocks?

We must relearn this tangible and visible practice of marking God's actions so we don't forget. Stones, when piled, are highly symbolic: they've been used to keep out enemy armies and mark boundaries between neighbors. But for the Israelites, stones were used to tell a story.

The kind of story that would remind Israel, and her children, and her children's children (us), what kind of God we serve.

See, the nature of piling stones is two fold: we look upon stones previous generations have piled in order to remember, but we also pile stones ourselves for future generations—thus a double nuance. We are called to remember and called to cause others to remember.

George Santayana said, "Those who cannot remember the past are condemned to repeat it." But as Christians we know those who do not remember the past may needlessly live in fear of the future. This is the message we pass on to those who will come after us: build for yourselves pillars declaring that there is a God who never fails, never leaves, never stops loving us, always takes care of us, and never forgets his promises.

talk

What are pivotal moments in your faith journey? What has God taught you in these times? And in what ways can the past teach you about tomorrow?

Our faith is shaped by the stones left by those who went before us. What stories of our ancestors are shaping us today? And how does it change the way we live to know that future generations depend on our stones of remembering?

_____

_____

_____

_____

# Dear God, it's me, Horace.

Sometimes God answers prayers in a day, but more often prayer is answered over a week, month, year, or even a lifetime. "The wind blows wherever it pleases. You hear its sound, but you cannot tell where it comes from or where it is going. So it is with everyone born of the Spirit" (John 3:8).

Begin tracking the Spirit of God by keeping a journal of short notes on the conversations you have with God. Review these notes periodically and see how God has answered prayers over time.

**Tell the page what you think.**

# Earth likes this. *green thumb up*

Be green with your memorial. (Yeah, we know you're *so* over The Garden chapter.) Instead of stacking stones like the Israelites, symbolize something God has done in your life or a promise he has fulfilled by planting a tree instead of stacking stones—when it grows put seating underneath and make it a place of shade, refuge, and solitude.

**Talk to me.**

# 1972 called, they want their mission back

If you think about it, your church is an altar of sorts—a bunch of stones, bricks, or wood stacked up really high because God wanted to do something in that place. Find out more about your church history. Why was it started? To meet what local needs? What was the mission then? And is it still being lived out?

**Tell the page what you think.**

# One cup of instant tears, please.

And since we're on the subject of stones, they're symbolic in other ways too. The Wailing Wall has been a Jewish landmark for centuries. One of the few remaining structures to survive Jerusalem's siege, this spot has been a sacred gathering place for mourning and prayer.

Maybe you'll have the opportunity to visit one day. But maybe not. In the meantime, build a small wall with your group and give people the chance to write their prayers and leave them between the stones.

**Word. (that's right, we know slang)**

# Eb-uh-nee-zer, word.

Buy a trunk or find an old wooden box, and begin to fill it with ebenezers or mementos of your story. Find creative ways to document the ways God has met with you and been faithful in the past.

**Drop a line.**

# rock on (and on, and on . . . )

Part of the reason Israel stacked stones was so the children would know
their story and be blessed by it for generations and generations to come.
Write out specific blessings, or find a blessing from Scripture this week
and share it with your children.

**Tell the page what you think.**

# We're kind of opposed to naked doors.

A Mezuzah is a blessing that hung on the doorframes of Jewish homes. Inscribed with Old Testament scripture, it was a reminder to pray. Traditionally, the Mezuzah contained text from Deuteronomy 6:4-9, "Hear, O Israel: The LORD our God, the LORD is one . . ."

Put something on your door, in your car, by your bed—somewhere where you will be reminded to rehearse a blessing. Perhaps the Jesus Prayer would be a good place to start: "Lord Jesus Christ, have mercy on me a sinner."

This kind of repetitious, contemplative prayer can be a way of communing with God throughout the day.

**Push a pencil.**

# Create your own experiment.

White spaces are meant to be filled, says us.

# the
# prophet

Deuteronomy 34:10-11

"Surely the Sovereign LORD does nothing without revealing his plan to his servants the prophets. The lion has roared—who will not fear? The Sovereign LORD has spoken—who can but prophesy?" (Amos 3:7-8).

You are a prophet. Seriously, you are. Before you get too giddy (or scared), you should know that being a prophet doesn't mean you can accurately predict the future. It also doesn't mean you need to start growing a huge, white beard and really long hair—think Charlton Heston in *The Ten Commandments*. No, that's (probably) not you.

However, if you are a part of God's huge movement called the Church— like it or not—you are a prophet. Simple as that.

Well maybe it's not *that* simple. Take for example one of the great human heroes of the Old Testament, Moses. (The guy we keep talking about.) Now there's a prophet.

**"Since then, no prophet has risen in Israel like Moses, whom the LORD knew face to face, who did all those miraculous signs and wonders the LORD sent him to do in Egypt—to Pharaoh and to all his officials and to his whole land" (Deuteronomy 34:10-11).**

He wasn't a prophet just because he threw down a stick that turned into a snake, or because he held up his hands to split the middle of a lake. Moses was a prophet because God told him to deliver a message to the Israelites, a far different message than the one they were getting from the Egyptians.

And different is the key.

For 400 years the Israelites had been slaves in Egypt, where they were told they were worth only the number of bricks they could produce. This was a lie. God called Moses to let the Israelites know they were his people and that he would take them out of Egypt to a place where they would be free. And Israel wasn't the only one who received this bit of information . . . God also called Moses to let the Egyptians know what was in the works. Moses was a prophet, a voice of good news (ahem, for some).

Moses was a prophet because he got in on God's vision to imagine and live out a far different world than the one the Israelites lived in at the time. The Israelites were slaves, but Moses said God was making them free. And that's exactly what a prophet is: one who can imagine, proclaim, and live out a different world than the world of the dominant culture.

So, you're a prophet. Actually, the Church is one big prophetic voice. As the Church, we imagine and live out a much different world than the oppressive and broken world of the dominant culture. Sounds intangible and distant, but it's not. It's exactly what Moses, all of the other OT prophets, and even Jesus did. In fact, Jesus had a name for this counterculture; he called it the kingdom of God (see Luke 4:16-21).

Egyptian oppression seems pretty foreign to us, but we're still enslaved. In our modern context slavery takes on all sorts of names.

Personally and corporately we may be slaves to debt, addiction, consumerism, pride, or anything that takes the place of God in our lives and eventually entraps. (Doesn't the spiritual always have very fleshy and tangible implications?)

And to make things real uncomfortable, slavery still exists on a literal level too—as in the complete bondage of human beings. In fact, there are a reported 27 million slaves today, which is more than at any other time in history.[4] This human trafficking takes various forms: forced child labor, sex slavery, debt bondage, child soldiers, and other dehumanizing practices.

It's almost as if this world needs the Church (a prophet) more than ever.

if you are neutral in situations of injustice, you have chosen the side of the oppressor. if an elephant has its foot on the tail of a mouse, and you say that you are neutral, the mouse will not appreciate your neutrality.

Desmond Tutu

A prophet is supposed to imagine with God and live out a different world than the world of dominant culture. Do Christians look different than the world in ways that really matter? How so?

talk

When Christ said, "It is finished," he really meant it. He won over death, slavery and all the other darknesses of this age—yet we don't always live in that reality. What are things that enslave you today?

# loudmouth, rejoice!

A prophet raises awareness. Dr. Cornel West said, "Justice is what love looks like in public."[5]

Let your love go public, and resist the urge to be apathetic by getting involved with group that needs your voice. Involvement has many faces: financial support, community service, or advocacy for a non-profit.

**Tell the page what you think.**

# *Now* you're speaking my language.

A prophet has a ministry of presence. As prophets, we must be proximal and really *live* amongst the people so we can know their language—for instance, how to speak and what to speak about.

It's hard to know the needs of your local community if you're never around, if you don't even know anyone's name.

Where do you get your coffee? What's your favorite restaurant? Instead of running in and out, get to know the people behind the counter. Call them by their first names. Be intentional about frequenting these places and building relationships.

**Drop a line.**

# Fact: Nightlights are not for wimps.

A prophet doesn't stay in the dark, though it's easier to sleep at night. Challenge yourself to become knowledgeable on some of the hard pressing issues going on in our world. Go to qideas.org and watch David Batstone's "Not for Sale." You can also visit callandresponse.com to educate yourself on local and global injustices.

**Push a pencil.**

# can't a person offer a tic tac without implying something?

A prophet wears weird clothes and eats weird food. Please see John the Baptist and Isaiah for examples.

We're not asking you to dress in camel's hair or run around naked (please don't), and have locust and honey for lunch (that's just asking for bad breath).

Instead, be a prophet of change by purchasing slave-free clothing. Or make it a point to buy fair trade chocolates and coffee. You'll find many more examples of conscious consumer choices in Julie Clawson's book, *Everyday Justice*.

**Tell the page what you think.**

# I pr@y n 140 charc+rs 0r l3ss.

A prophet is contemplative. Praying is about listening for God's will. These people didn't just randomly pick a cause; they were quiet before the Lord and asked him to reveal the places he was working in the world.

This week turn off your social mediums.
Your radio.
Your TV.
Your iPod.
Your computer.
Your books on tape.

And pray. (By that we mean listen.)

**Do tell.**

# Hi there best-thing-ever.

A prophet has a thankless job. Make contact with someone who is leading a social justice cause, and personally thank them for their work. Find out their story—why do they dedicate their lives to this work? Could be inspiring.

**Word. (that's right, we know slang)**

# ignoring the elephant in the room (and the donkey for that matter).

A prophet has a different politic. Many of the things we demand from our government—taking care of the poor (welfare), healing the sick (healthcare), providing for the foreigner (immigration)—are things we've been called to do as a Church.

This week, reflect: What sort of things am I asking government to do in terms of education, ecology, healthcare, poverty, etc. that the Church should also be taking steps to address?

This isn't about Democrat or Republican; this is about the role of the faith community. Report back.

**Tell the page what you think.**

# Create your own experiment.

Do Tell.

the
fields

Leviticus 19:9-10

I really don't hoard all that much. Granted, I can't seem to let go of those eight pairs of kicks I have in my closet, but that's more of a fashion issue. And my overstocked pantry? Clearly you didn't live through Y2K; I've been prepared ever since. And concerning those storage units I filled up a few years ago? *Shoulder Shrug* I couldn't just give that stuff away, right?

Alright, maybe I've let my savings account get a little fat. Maybe I have a tendency to store up possessions for myself. And maybe I can't remember all the codes for all the locks that secure all my things for a time when I'll actually use them. . . . Whew, I'm certainly not alone. (It's just hard to count guilty heads when we're all buried under piles of stuff.)

Living in the wealthiest nation to date, stockpiling has become somewhat of a societal norm. We even give it a noble name like "security." And yet we know when we consume at the expense of others, this is not God's intention for blessing us so richly.

The Israelites had stockpiling tendencies too. That's why throughout the Old Testament, God was constantly sending messengers to remind the Israelites that the Promised Land—and all that milk and honey—wasn't theirs to take ownership over. They hadn't received the land and its rich harvest because they had somehow earned the buying rights, but instead because God had delighted to give them a gift.

In response to the blessing, he asked Israel to live generously: **"When you reap the harvest of your land, do not reap to the very edges of your field or gather the gleanings of your harvest. Do not go over your vineyard a second time or pick up the grapes that have fallen. Leave them for the poor and the alien. I am the LORD your God"** (Leviticus 19:9-10).

This was God's way of saying, "Hey, remember when you were once poor and foreign yourselves, living in a land where the inhabitants did not care for you? And remember when I took you out from under that oppression so you could experience a different kind of humanity? Yeah, well, you should probably just share some of your grapes before they turn into raisins."

Hoarding is not only harmful to the community, something happens when we posture our hearts toward consumption. We begin using the words "mine" and "yours" and meaning it. We find ourselves living and dying by the boundary lines of our fields.

In other words, we begin to take on earthly citizenship.

But when the people of Israel practiced self-restraint and allowed the marginalized to glean from their fields, they were declaring citizenship to an eternal kingdom. They were embodying the image of God—receiving blessings for the sake of blessing others. They were claiming nothing as their own—refusing to take ownership.

Now let's fast-forward to today. What would happen if this were our prayer? Let us not forget that the Church is to be good news for the poor and alien. And that we are the poor and alien ourselves. Let us not forget that the Church is called to remember where we came from and act in such a way that the memory is lived out. Let us not forget that the Church extends around the world—without boundary lines or one form of government. Let us not forget *why* we've received the kingdom.

The Promised Land.

The fields.

if we had any possessions, we should need weapons and laws to defend them.

**St. Francis**

**talk**

In God's economy no one "owns" anything, but he entrusts us with the distribution of his resources. In your opinion, when we live in surplus, are we stealing from those in need? Why or why not?

Be honest: how do you feel about the idea of gleaning, and what do you think that practice might look like today?

# Research shows: we're trashy.

Extra waste.

Compost your garbage instead of throwing it all away. Over 60 percent of household waste is fit for compost. Not only are you not throwing more stuff away, but you will also be providing needed nutrients for your soil! Google search: "What can I compost?" to find out more.

Also, keep track of everything you throw away this week. Reconfigure your consumption habit so you can waste less and give more. When we read this it made us sick to our stomachs:

"New York City alone has an annual surplus of about 50 million pounds of food. Ten years ago, the United States Department of Agriculture estimated that more than 96 billion pounds of edible food went to waste. And, according to anthropologist Tim Jones, the United States throws away just about half of the food it produces."[6]

**Save the ink industry. (Write things down.)**

# your room is ~~board~~ bored.

Extra rooms.

Consider what your church is using its space for throughout the week. What about allowing an organization to use your facilities? Or personally, reflect on the additional space you have within your home—a finished basement could be the perfect place for a youth event, or a spare bedroom could host an exchange student.

Donate some of your square footage to a·good cause.

**Tell the page what you think.**

# Think Internet, but from a tree.

Extra books.

Stories have a way of shaping our realities, and education has given people opportunities to imagine a new future for themselves. Donate some of your books to a local charity, prison ministry, or public library.

And if you're a real Dr. Seuss fanatic, consider tutoring or volunteering at an after-school reading program.

**Word. (that's right, we know slang)**

# Garage sale = garage fail (campaign brought to you by your exiled car).

Extra things.

Prepare as if you were having a garage sale, but give it away instead. Simplify. Doesn't the rule go if you haven't used something in three months, then it's out? Distribute to an urban charity. Another option is to post your stuff on Craigslist under the "free" section.

**White spaces are meant to be filled, says us.**

# the shelter briefing.

Extra clothes.

Rather than going shopping for the upcoming season, arrange a clothing exchange within your group of friends.

Or drop off your excess at a homeless shelter. Maybe you didn't know it, but the largest need for most shelters are the "unmentionables." We're talking underwear and socks, etc. So instead of shopping in your closet for those (like, gross), you may want to go the store and purchase new ones.

**Tell the page what you think.**

# The dollar is—how do we say it?—having a midlife crisis.

Extra change.

A dollar isn't worth what it once was, but we're convinced that loose change can still add up. Put all your spare chump (translation: coins) in a can. At the end of the month count it, double it, and ask God where he wants it to go.

**Pen, say hello to paper.**

# The blue collar, the white collar, and the anti-collar.

Extra labor.

We know you already give 40 hours a week to your job, to sharpening your skills, to developing your craft. Why not use your expertise for the community? Instead of donating money, employ your skills for someone else's good.

A community option includes creating a board where people can write down both needs they have and services they can offer. For instance:

An electrician? Maybe there is a family who lives in an underprivileged neighborhood and needs some light.

Work at home mom? Help run errands for someone who is housebound.

A barista? Serve some good coffee at a volunteer event.

**Tell the page what you think.**

# create your own experiment.

Tell the page what you think.

the

pilgrim

Deuteronomy 16:16a

I'm such a sojourner.

I journey exactly 37 minutes to work every morning—that is, if traffic is moving. Occasionally I take the parking space that's a little farther back so I can meet my daily step quota. And one summer when I really wanted to be intentional about this journey thing, I traveled all the way to a beach resort in San Diego by way of Southwest Airlines.

Some might call that a vacation.

But only because they've never had to endure a four-hour flight sitting next to a hipster who stopped wearing deodorant circa the late '90s and wanted to share his entire iTunes library of experimental music.

Okay, so I don't get this pilgrimage thing that the Israelites faithfully practiced. It doesn't have context in a world where my GPS is set to the fastest route. Besides, pilgrimage has been somewhat dismissed in the Western, Evangelical Church. Lumped in somewhere between disciplines and the sacraments, we've written it off as too ancient, too mystical, and if nothing else—too impractical.

But perhaps it's worth revisiting. And here's why.

Pilgrimage has its roots in the Exodus narrative. You know the story by now:

A nation enslaved.

Our guy Moses as an unlikely leader.

Some ocean-splitting action.

. . . This story was their identity—God proclaiming them free in a world that had named them slaves.

And so the first month of every year Israel and her descendents intentionally reenacted the journey of God moving them from captivity to liberation.

For our ancestors this looked like a road trip to Jerusalem to celebrate the Feast of the Passover, which was one of the most important religious events on their calendar. For those coming from the outlying areas, the trip could take more than a week.

And Passover wasn't the only time in the year they made this journey: **"*Three* times a year all your men must appear before the LORD your God at the place he will choose: at the Feast of Unleavened Bread, the Feast of Weeks and the Feast of Tabernacles." (Deuteronomy 16:16a,** emphasis added**).**

The question stands—why all the travel?

God's metanarrative is one of redeeming the world. But with all sorts of competing god stories, we tend to forget what he's up to, and thus our participation in his redemptive work.[7]

But in pilgrimage we find an identity. We move forward. Pilgrimage keeps us from wandering.

The Psalmist says it like this: "Blessed are those whose strength is in you, who have set their hearts on pilgrimage. As they pass through the Valley of Baca [tears], they make it a place of springs; the autumn rains also cover it with pools. They go from strength to strength, till each appears before God in Zion" (Psalm 84:5-7).

The imagery here is profound—our tears refresh us? Something happens to us when we set apart time and space for the purpose of remembering where we came from and where we are headed. We are transformed as we walk with God on a trajectory that will lead us to knowing him more. That means the journey is every bit as important as the destination.

Even Jesus uses all sorts of journey language that would have ignited the Jews' imagination around exodus. "Follow me!" (Matthew 4:19a) and "I am the *way*, the truth and the life" (John 14:6, emphasis added).

And as a final plug, it's important to note that pilgrimage isn't primarily about the individual journey—about making the hike alone. Part of knowing God is knowing the people around us, so don't go off trying to find your own way.

In a place where most of us have always lived as "free," it's easy to question whether pilgrimage is necessary. What or where is your Egypt from which you've escaped? What might a pilgrimage journey look like for you?

_____

_____

talk

God's narrative is one of redeeming the world, and it's important that we set apart time and space to remember this. What are the competing god stories that fight for our attention and affection?

# Thanksgiving every day, cause we heart grandma's gravy.

Gratitude journey.

This week flip your prayer time upside down. Spend twice as much time thanking God as you do asking for stuff. Make a gratitude journal if you want to document things along the way.

**Word. (that's right, we know slang)**

# Jesus went into a desert (hence the sandbox in my backyard).

Solitude journey.

Take a one-day retreat over the weekend. Go somewhere where you can find solitude: a campsite, a monastery, a hiking trail . . . somewhere quiet. Spend time reflecting on where you have been over the past year and where you think God is leading you in the year ahead. When you get home, share what God has revealed so you can encourage one another throughout the coming months.

**Tell the page what you think.**

# the saint, the ma, and the rev (no punch line here).

Saintly journey.

Pick a saint or leader in the Christian Church and study his or her habits and practices of spiritual discipline. Some of our favorites? Saint Francis of Assisi—he was an environmentalist before it was cool. Ma Theresa—she went to the slums with her theology. Or Reverend Martin Luther King Jr.—non-violent protesting was his thing.

**Tell the page what you think.**

# Shut your yapper.

Journey of silence.

Barbara Brown Taylor says that to speak is to exhale solitude.[8] Go twelve hours without speaking. Begin this experiment when you wake up. What are your observations about the day?

**Drop a line.**

# Talking to God—yeah, there's an app for that.

Scriptural journey.

As a means of rehearsing our Biblical story, pray a Psalm morning, noon, and night this week.

After this week if you want to start on a journey of liturgical prayer, check out the Book of Common Prayer or the Daily Office. (And we were being serious . . .you can download the Daily Office application to your iPhone if you're real techy and what not.)

**Save the ink industry. (Write things down.)**

# compassion fatigue.

Compassion journey.

Often our churches have much further to go in the way of caring for local communities. As a group, get in touch with one of the social workers in your city and ask for your church to be put on a need-basis contact list. This means your church will be called upon to answer local needs as they arise. Work to maintain this partnership throughout the long haul.

**Tell the page what you think.**

# This is a state of emergency: stop buying skinny jeans.

Journey of simplicity.

Part of setting apart time and space might mean to de-clutter your life in terms of consumption. Try going an entire month without buying any new "wants" (remembering that we can always justify "wants" as "needs").

See if you can go a month with no new clothes, DVDs, video games, books, or anything you don't *really* need. Be generous with the money saved, and anonymously give it to someone in need.

**Self-published = write in this book.**

# Create your own experiment.

Save the ink industry. (Write things down.)

the

goat

Leviticus 16:20-22

Growing up our family friends the Millers had a crotchety old goat named Naomi. She didn't really like anyone with the exception of one of the Miller girls. (Why is it that girls always have each other's backs?) One time she even butted me off a rock wall. I really didn't like that goat. And the fact that I can still recall the goat's name a decade later is testament to that.

The Israelites had goat problems too: scapegoat problems. Once a year a priest would bring a goat—among other sacrifices and rituals—and placing his hands on the scapegoat, he would lay all the sins of Israel on its head. Then they would turn the goat loose into the desert and it would symbolically carry with it the sins of the people **(Leviticus 16:20-22)**.

Kind of a wild scene, right?

But that's just it. It wasn't something the participants would soon forget:

> *Hey, remember when we sent that goat into the wilderness?*

> *Huh? Don't recall that . . .*

(Yeah, right.)

And it wasn't just goats that served as a visual reminder; it seems like the Israelites were constantly interacting with God inside visual narratives of repentance—building altars, sacrificing livestock, fasting, observing religious holidays. The list goes on and on . . .

But we've got to know, what was the offense? Why were they always so sorry?

Thousands of years ago Moses walked down from a mountain with some words from God—the Ten Commandments. They contained prohibitions against all sorts of sin: adultery, murder, theft, jealousy, idolatry. The

Scripture tells us that those rules were written on tablets of stone and that no one was righteous in light of these commands—all had turned away from their covenant relationship (Psalm 53:2-3).

And so we fast-forward to find that God had a more redemptive word for his people and that Christ would write a new law on tablets of flesh—our hearts (Ezekiel 36:26-27, Jeremiah 31:33).

But Christ's remix of the law doesn't make it easier on us. He took "don't kill" and said, "don't hate." He took "don't commit adultery" and said, "don't even look at someone lustfully." Admit it, any time Jesus is in the picture, things get more uncomfortable by the minute. This law isn't just difficult, it's *impossible* to keep.

Which may be the point.

God doesn't want us to live in sin; he wants us to obey his commands. After all, they teach us how to live in our bodies better and how to exist well with each other. However, the law was also written to show us that we are absolutely incapable of keeping it. Our own frailty and complete desperate need drive us to God.

God's first intention for humanity was that we would live in dynamic relationship with him. It's not his desire that sin *or guilt* keep us away. Sure there are consequences for our choices, but in Christ we are made completely new. The old is gone and all is made new. Not part, not half, not what we want—all. God cleanses our sins and removes our condemnation.

Begin living in a new era of the goat.

Not a scapegoat of blaming shortcomings on others, but of turning over your life to Christ completely—letting sorrow loose into the desert.

What would it look like if we let grace be the most transformative process in our lives? If we became a merciful people? It's not a feel-good gospel, it's one of the most provocative and demanding calls on our lives: "Forgive us our debts, as we also have forgiven our debtors . . ." (Matthew 6:12).

# talk

As Christians we're called to forgive and love not only our friends (Jesus said even sinners can do that) but also our enemies. Yet complete forgiveness may sometimes feel impossible. Is forgiveness more than a feeling? Using the scenarios discussed above, how do you resist the temptation to call those goats back from the wilderness?

_____

_____

We often separate grace as something different from faith. Are they? When we refuse to believe grace is making us blameless before God, what does that say about our faith in Christ—or his ability to justify?

———————

# no, it's totally normal (weird) that you still suck your thumb.

Get rid of a bad habit.

**Tell the page what you think.**

# Maybe I have a pedometer and pretend like it's a pager.

The prayer walk.

We all know people who carry guilt from a past mistake. Walk seven times around your house, your place of work, or your church and pray specifically for co-workers, family members, and friends that you know are carrying around the burden of past sin. Pray for peace.

**White spaces are meant to be filled, says us.**

# Gotta get your soul to the dry cleaners.

We're pretty private about our soiled pasts and our track records. But our testimonies are one of the most powerful confessions we have of God at work. Write out your testimony and review it. When the opportunity presents itself, be ready to tell the story of how God is drawing you into relationship with himself.

**Word. (that's right, we know slang)**

# can it.

There's something profound about the fact the Israelites would sacrifice things that provided them sustenance (livestock and grain offerings) for the sake of community righteousness.

As a group, make a commitment to fast a meal together. With the money saved from that meal, buy or prepare a meal for someone who could really use it.

**Tell the page what you think.**

# You really get my goat.

You've been given grace. Your shame has been taken away, driven into the desert, nailed to the cross. Who are you refusing to forgive? This week spend some time in quiet and begin to release those feelings of bitterness toward others.

And for that matter, Christ not only calls us to forgive our enemies, he calls us to go the extra mile for them. Remember the story about turning the other cheek? About giving up our coat when someone has only asked for our shirt (Luke 6)? So, this week brainstorm how you can actually bless that person who offended you and seek to be reconciled with them.

**Push a pencil.**

# For the birds.

God's forgiven you, but you haven't forgiven yourself quite yet. Releasing a goat into the wild could be a big fat mess—besides, we think it may be illegal. But there are other ways to symbolize release: type out your guilt in a Word document, then erase it. Buy a dove at the pet store, and let it go. Make a bonfire (well, not if you live in California).

We don't care, just be creative and tell us how it went.

**Pen, say hello to paper.**

# forgivenomics.

Forgiveness works both ways. Spend time in prayer and ask God to reveal someone you've wronged—someone you need to be reconciled with. Seek out that person you have offended in the past and attempt to give restitution for your wrong.

**Tell the page what you think.**

# Create your own experiment.

Save the ink industry. (Write things down.)

# the stranger

Genesis 18:1-15

I mean, what's a patriarch to do? Three strangers show up at his tent unannounced, without even bothering to make a reservation. Uh, rude. And what does the Lord require of Abraham? Hospitality.

In so much of our world today, strangers are considered a risk. So we send them off with a couple bucks. Or to a motel. Or to social services. Anywhere considered a safe distance away from us. It seems we have feelings of guilt when it comes to socializing with strangers. On one hand, we want to be welcoming like Jesus, but on the other hand—ugh. What if we bring a visitor into our home and he eats the last Pop-Tart, or worse?

In the Biblical narrative, hospitality had nothing to do with the Martha Stewart manner of entertaining friends and family like we often think today. Instead, it was "the process of 'receiving' outsiders and changing them from strangers to guests."[9]

The ancient rules of hospitality are splattered all over the Scriptures. However, one of the more visible manifestations of hospitality involved Abraham, Sarah, and their three visitors. (Want the whole story? Take a look at **Genesis 18:1-15**). The story goes that God showed up in the form of three men while Abraham chilled out on today's equivalent of a front porch. And though he didn't know it, these guys were bringing some news about:

A baby.

A lineage that would continue forever.

A kingdom where God would establish his throne.

(You know, your average small talk.)

Even before Abraham knew about any of this, his cultural hospitality code kicked in. He bowed to honor them, sent for food and water, made sure their feet got washed, and invited them to rest with him under some oak trees.

But this story wasn't perfect.

If you read on, you see that Abraham was gracious in receiving his guests but didn't completely receive their words; at one point both he and Sarah had a good chuckle when they were told they would have a son. They are quick to share food, but not faith.

There's something to learn here about the difference in hospitality and entertainment. Perhaps true hospitality contains a faith element?

After all, there are spiritual implications for our hospitality toward others. Maybe every stranger we invite into our lives carries a bit of "news" about who God is and what he's up to. C.S. Lewis says something similar: "There are no *ordinary* people. You have never talked to a mere mortal . . . Next to the Blessed Sacrament itself, your neighbour is the holiest object presented to your senses."[10]

We give of ourselves because God has given so much to us. And it's not a matter of sitting around our houses, waiting for someone to drop by. Hospitality is the intentional practice of caring for people, turning strangers into friends, and welcoming the kingdom.

For instance, look around you right now. What would happen if you began eating with these people? Serving with these people? Living near these people? An hour on Sunday morning might not do the trick.

But we caution you, with community comes real accountability and vulnerability. It sometimes (always) gets messy.

On the flip side, you might just find the kingdom.

our job is to love others without stopping to inquire whether or not they are worthy. that is not our business and, in fact, it is nobody's business. what we are asked to do is to love, and this love itself will render both ourselves and our neighbors worthy.

171

**Thomas Merton**

We are made in the image of God—and we all embody something unique to that image. Do you believe it? In what ways do we act (or not act) like others are as holy as "the Blessed Sacraments" themselves?

talk

It's hard to turn strangers into friends when we isolate ourselves behind gated communities and privacy walls. Are we present and available to the poor and needy stranger? Are we even in places where we can give uncomfortable hospitality?

---

# Talking to my neighbor? Uh, do I get community service hours for that?

Sharing resources.

Do others see you as a good neighbor? Hint: try asking them! Look for ways to offer your time or resources to those immediately around you. Are there any neighbors you haven't met yet? Invite them over for a meal.

**Tell the page what you think.**

# jalopy love.

Sharing transportation.

It's pretty hard to imagine life without mobility, but lots of folks are restricted. Visit a local nursing home and see if you can help one of the residents run errands or go out on the town. Check out a concert, ballgame, special church service, good movie, or the local farmer's market.

**Tell the page what you think.**

# Made with love (and a bunch of Crisco).

Sharing food.

As Christians we should be good at throwing parties! Make a group commitment to have community meals more often. Make it a time of intentional hospitality toward one another. The Israelites began their festivities/holidays at sundown—conveniently right about the time dinner started. They seemed to grasp the importance of feast.

Perhaps you can discuss with your pastor an experiment of gathering on a Saturday night instead of Sunday morning once this month.

**Pen, say hello to paper.**

# bread and wine (evangelical remix: wafer and grape juice).

Sharing sacraments.

For centuries, the Eucharist has been a measure of inviting all to the table of Christ to commune with God and one another. Next time you meet as a small group, ask an ordained minister to lead your group in this sacrament. Prepare by giving a brief history of the Eucharist and by reading I Corinthians 11:23-26.

Talk about ways you can implement the sacraments in your church community.

**Tell the page what you think.**

# so much class it hurts.

Sharing art.

You knew we were going to get all artsy and highbrow on you eventually.

Andrei Rublev painted a beautiful icon, *The Hospitality of Abraham*, which portrayed this scene from Genesis. Find a copy of it and check out the history behind the art. What was Rublev trying to say about God's hospitality?

**Save the ink industry. (Write things down.)**

# But mum told me not to talk to strangers.

Sharing church.

Does your church environment seem to welcome others or caution them to keep their distance? Are the conversations taking place there a source of invitation or exclusion?

This Sunday, choose someone you don't know (perhaps someone new to your community) and invite them to coffee, to your small group, or to an activity. Make this an exchange you follow up with.

Something to think about as a group: how can your church body rearrange its habits so guests will be truly welcomed?

**White spaces are meant to be filled, says us.**

# Schooled.

Sharing study.

You look forward to Sunday mornings, but maybe you want to grow spiritually with your community from Monday to Saturday. One way to do this involves collectively reading through the Bible and/or formational books throughout the weekday. There's something powerful about learning together in this way.

**Tell the page what you think.**

# create your own experiment.

Drop a line.

# Endnotes

1 David Cannell, "Lose the Cattle, Save the World," *GOOD*, May 8, 2009, http://www.good.is/post/lose-the-cattle-save-the-world.

2 Adam Matthews and Siobhan O'Connor, "This Is A Turn Off: the *GOOD* Guide to Reducing Your Water Use," *GOOD*, July 28, 2009, http://www.good.is/post/this-is-a-turn-off.

3 *UnChristian* official Web site, "UnChristian Data Summary," http://www.unchristian.com/downloads/uc_data.pdf (accessed December 20, 2009).

4 *Call and Response*, directed by Justin Dillon (Oakland, CA: Fair Trade Pictures, 2008).

5 *Call and Response*, directed by Justin Dillon (Oakland, CA: Fair Trade Pictures, 2008).

6 Peter Smith, "The United States is a Food Wasteland," *GOOD,* October 22,2009, http://www.good.is/post/the-united-states-is-a-food-wasteland.

7 Tim Keel, *The Practice of Pilgrimage*, audio files of lectures from Jacob's Well Church, Kansas City, MO, August 12, 2007, http://www.jacobswellchurch.org/sermon_audio (accessed December 1, 2009).

8 Barbara Brown Taylor, *When God is Silent* (Lanham, MD: Cowley, 1998).

9 John J. Pilch and Bruce J. Malina, *Biblical Social Values and Their Meaning: A Handbook* (Peabody, MA: Hendrickson, 1993).

10 C. S. Lewis, *The Weight of Glory* (New York: HarperCollins, 1949).

# the kingdom experiment

A Community Practice on Intentional Living

thekingdomexperiment.com

dawning of the new beard